D0287947

The Wit & Wisdom of West Highland Terriers

This edition is created for LOMOND

FLAME TREE
6 Melbray Mews
Fulham, London SW6 3NS
United Kingdom
www.flametreepublishing.com

First edition published 2007

17 19 20 18
3 5 7 9 10 8 6 4 2

© Flame Tree Publishing Ltd 2015

The right of Ulysses Brave to be identified as the author of this work has been asserted by him in accordance with the Copyright, Designs and Patents Act 1988.

All rights reserved. No part of this publication may be reproduced or transmitted, in any form or by any means, without the prior permission in writing of the publisher.

The CIP record for this book is available from the British Library.

ISBN: 978 1 84204 487 2

Printed in China

Thanks to: Cat Taylor, Sara Robson and Gemma Walters

The Wit & Wisdom of West Highland Terriers

Ulysses Brave

LOMOND

Foreword

For years I studied Zen and the Art of Animal Self-consciousness. Subsequently I have written a large number of management, self-help and philosophical texts over the years, which have provided useful advice and inspiration. Here then, is the latest offering.

Ulysses Brave

Inner calm is a rare, often unrecognized quality.

Confidence is the key to success. When hunting for friends or jobs, always walk with a ready smile and a straight back.

Try to avoid situations which you find depressing.

Make some time every
day to celebrate.

Fear is your greatest enemy. You can defeat it by remembering those who love you.

If you have trouble concentrating, just take five deep breaths and remain still for two minutes.

Be ready for action at all times, especially in the defence of your places of rest.

Sometimes the perfect colour
is simply not available.
Try not to put yourself
under too much pressure.

Don't feel ashamed about the silly things you do in the privacy of your own home.

Twins can be fun!

Curiosity can be a good thing.
Judgement is always better.

If life seems to become entangled, try to do something completely different.

There are times when we all want to sink into the background. Camouflage, correctly administered, can be useful.

Here we go again...

Opening your lungs first thing in the morning will fill your body with life-enhancing energy.

The ancient art of moon-staring can bring significant benefits to the inner soul.

Luxuries and privileges can sometimes hold you back. It is often better to fight for what you want.

Just focus on your goals...

...dont wait for events, leap towards them and wrestle them to the ground.

Going to a party can relieve the tension, even if it's the last thing you want to do.

Some people like parties!

Try to maintain a healthy diet.

If you bring a friend to an important event, make sure they don't cramp your style.

Watch and compose yourself before you leap in. Success lies in planning and poise.

Dreaming of a better place can help you through the day.

Sometimes it's a great relief to get to the end of the day.

Keep your spine in a neutral position for as long as you can manage.

Try to leave the city behind for a few hours a week.

Some people will be wary if you show too much enthusiasm.

Try to find a new
challenge in your life.

If you find yourself in a tight corner, genuine curiosity can be the most disarming weapon.

All forms of Martial Arts provide great discipline.

You know a true friend by their attitude to your appearance.

See you soon ...